A TREASURY of
Inspired Poems

Edward J. McCoul

WESTBOW
PRESS®
A DIVISION OF THOMAS NELSON
& ZONDERVAN

WestBow Press books may be ordered through booksellers or by contacting:

WestBow Press
A Division of Thomas Nelson & Zondervan
1663 Liberty Drive
Bloomington, IN 47403
www.westbowpress.com
1 (866) 928-1240

ISBN: 978-1-5127-2849-1 (sc)

Library of Congress Control Number: 2016901349

Print information available on the last page.

WestBow Press rev. date: 03/21/2016

"A Special Thank You"

I want to give a special thank you to, Diane, a great artist. She puts so much love for The Lord into her art. It is such an honor to have her beautiful artwork grace the interior of my book.

Contents

"Trust and Obey"

Lord, I trust in Your understanding.
I obey You without my planning.
I live for You daily wholeheartedly.
Your love never parts from me!

The Light of Your Presence is real.
Its reassurance I yearn to feel.
It gives me continual reinforcement.
Your Light, I trust for my fulfillment!

I trust not in my thinking that's frail.
Compared to Your Word it does pale.
I obey and follow You all of my days,
Blessed on Earth and in Heaven always!

You are my God, my Heavenly Father.
I submit to You as Your loving Son.
Jesus is my guiding Light, no other.
We trust and obey and it is done!

In The Bible all Your promises are true.
I claim them by faith trusting in You.
I obey what's in Your life-giving Word,
The most beautiful words I ever heard!

Jesus showed the best example of trust
By obeying His Father and dying for us.
We trust and die to self by obeying Him.
It's the way we show love again and again!

I trust that I can share this Good News.
If I do not share, many lives may lose.
"Let His Light shine before it is too late.
Let's trust and obey," I lovingly state!

"Onward Christian Soldier"

In case you are unaware
It's a spiritual war out there.
Everyday pray and prepare.
Don accoutrements with care!

Lord, anoint me and so I pray:
"A Helmet of Salvation be on today.
With it keep my mind renewed.
Temptations do not come through!

I want to be your Christian Soldier.
Let me wear what makes me bolder.
Breastplate of Righteousness, protect.
The enemy's attacks help me reject!

Your anointing be upon both my feet
To spread the gospel without defeat.
Let me tell wonderful things about You.
It is what a soldier in your army must do!

Every encounter has a moment of truth.
Let me show love, not 'tooth for tooth.'
I will wield The Sword of the Spirit.
The world, flesh, and devil fear it!"

If you prepare, failure will have no place.
Jesus' Grace has saved the human race.
A Christian Soldier must walk in that Light.
In that anointing it will be easy to do right!

Christian Soldiers endure to the last.
Walk in the Godly ways of men past.
Good men of the future will walk in yours,
Their eyes on Jesus whom they adore!

"Leave No Man Behind"

As Christians, God's aim we seek to find.
An aim for sure is to leave no man behind.
We speak of Jesus' love to those we greet,
Inviting them to The Lamb's Wedding Feast!

The invitation has been sent by God above,
Who sent His Son to die for us out of His love.
We must sow the words of faith along life's path,
Saying, "Jesus is the way to avoid God's wrath!

Life is a battlefield filled with the hurting and lost.
Spread the Gospel of Hope not counting the cost.
The people that the Lord leads you daily to find
May thank Jesus forever for not being left behind!

Life is short and its worldly diversions are plenty.
The enemy's snares entangle and deceive many.
In Christ we have victory, for He is the true Way.
Our sins on Calvary's Cross for us He did pay!

Not all words take root in the hearts of lost men,
But many who hear of Him willingly start again.
They make Jesus their Lord, adhering to Him,
Having been told the truth with no 'worldly spin!'

Greet every man and woman with the Good News,
Telling as though that person could have been you.
Love is gentle. Love is patient. Love is always kind.
So, my friends in Christ, "Leave No Man Behind!"

"Good Morning, Lord"

Good morning, Lord, how is Your new day?
Good morning, Lord, with me please stay.

Good morning, Lord, I love being with You.
Good morning, Lord, show me what to do.

Good morning, Lord, birds greet The King.
Good morning, Lord, for you birds do sing.

Good morning, Lord, are miracles in store?
Good morning, Lord, it is You that I adore.

Good morning, Lord, planets rotate for You.
Good morning, Lord, sun's glow, You renew.

Good morning, Lord, You see ocean floors.
Good morning, Lord, all nations are Yours.

Good morning, Lord, You number the stars.
Good morning, Lord, All say, "Here we are"

Good morning, Lord, flowers You do grow.
Good morning, Lord, all the trees You know.

Good morning, Lord, We love Your Grace.
Good morning, Lord, in Light we keep pace.

Good morning, Lord, I am ready to begin.
Good morning, Lord, in You, I win, win, win.

So a new day let us begin again and again,
Again, again, and... again. Together we win!

"Sweet Hour of Prayer"

That sweet hour of prayer is here.
It's those moments that I hold dear.
It is when Your sweet Spirit is near.
In Your Presence everything is clear!

In that hour I will know what to do.
It is just part of my clinging to You.
Every hour brings a time to renew
With prayers that I offer up to You!

A sweet, sweet Spirit fills that hour.
As I enter into Your freeing power.
I am safe in You, Jesus, My Tower,
In that Grace-Filled Sweetest Hour!

You inspire me with words to pray
As I seek to please You, Your way.
Grace makes praying seem like play
In those 24 sweet hours of every day!

Sweet hour of prayer came with cost.
It is part of Your salvation for the lost.
You brought freedom to us at the Cross.
Resurrection's Gold refines any dross!

So in that sweet hour I pray and wait.
Prayers go fast past Heaven's Gate.
They are answered hourly, never late,
In that sweet hour from Your Godly Estate!

I will never stop praying continually.
It comes from my heart unceasingly.
I pray, in Sweet Jesus, most pleasingly.
Thanks in that hour for redeeming me!

"I Know"

I know my Jesus loves me so.
His Grace covers me head to toe.
He is my bright Morning Star.
His love for me is never far.

Being God's chosen makes me glad.
With God's love I am never sad.
He fills my day with joy.
I am one Spirit-filled boy.

I am sharing this with the world.
His joy is a banner of love unfurled.
I know His love is sweet to behold.
I know Jesus' Hand I will always hold.

His Resurrection Power is like gold.
It surrounds me 'til I am good and old!
Being with Him is a dream come true.
It is not just for me, but also for you.

Faith in Him will see you through.
He died for me and also for you.
He gave His life not counting the cost.
So go share His love with the lost.

"Friends in Christ"

Friends in Christ are the best.
They stand out from the rest.
Jesus' Blood has washed them.
They grow in stature, holy in Him.

These are the people chosen.
For whom He died and rose again.
This isn't a make-believe story.
He did rise and went to His Glory.

He did this because He loves us.
Can anyone understand the Cross?
I love Him dearly and that is that.
I bow before You on the floor flat.

I am not messing around with Truth.
My faith in You has established roots.
For my new life You are the reason.
That's why I praise You in any season.

You are my closest Friend forever
Because of Your Love, not my endeavor.
I give my all to be connected to You.
Your love has saved me out of the blue.

In the world I seek my family in Christ
They are friends in Spirit not sight.
Together we bond and uphold You.
What a blessed holy thing it is to do.

Friends in Christ are the best.
They stand out from the rest.
Jesus' Blood has washed them.
We grow in stature, holy in Him.

"Your Word"

Your Word is Jesus.
Your Word dwelt among us.
Your Word calms the tempest.
Your Word in It, we invest.

Your Word is a Holy Thing.
Your Word makes angels sing.
Your Word is Love in Action.
Your Word is Pure Satisfaction.

Your Word is the only Soul-Fixer.
Your Word is a Marvelous Elixir.
Your Word reaches the unsaved.
Your Word makes men brave.

Your Word is a Beautiful Beacon.
Your Word attracts those seek'n.
Your Word scatters the darkness.
Your Word is Love and Kindness.

Your Word is an Untiring Fountain.
Your Word moves any mountain.
Your Word was made Flesh.
Your Word enables starting fresh.

Your Word is self-perpetuating.
Your Word has stopped debating.
Your Word shines without end.
Your Word to man, God did send.

Your Word breaks death's seal.
Your Word is Eternal Life revealed.
Your Word is a Public Treasure.
Your Word is Life Without Measure.

Your Word brings abundant change.
Your Word makes lives rearrange.
Your Word is One Who gave.
Your Word rose from the tomb-cave.

Your Word relieves the thirst of men.
Your Word was before time began.
Your Word is multiplied by the wind.
Your Word frees those who've sinned.

Your Word gives wings to Truth.
Your Word dispels ignorance, forsooth.
Your Word is The Living Water.
Your Word saves sons and daughters.

Your Word is a Spring of Truth so Pure.
Your Word throughout time will endure.
Your Word is like a Radiant Sunbeam.
Your Word flows in inexhaustible streams.

Your Word is multiplied like the wind.
Your Word saves those who have sinned.
Your Word was once an unknown light.
Your Word is The Light, Heaven's Delight.

"He 'Rocks' My World"

The Rock of my life 'rocks' my life.
He keeps my world in its place.
My days with Him are free of strife.
In my heart He has a sacred space.

We are on a rock orbiting the sun.
I revolve around the Chosen One.
He keeps heavenly bodies in corridors.
My world in Him moves in perfect order.

If you see me going down the street,
It is He and I that you will greet.
We will greet you with a kind smile.
That blessed response is on redial.

With Him I move at a different beat.
He keeps me cool through the 'heat.'
I love doing different things with Him.
He sticks by me through thick or thin.

The Rock of my life 'rocks' my life.
He keeps my world in its place.
My days with Him are free of strife.
In my heart He has a sacred space.

"God's Little Flower"

I am just God's little flower.
He grows me hour by hour.
Right now I am 24 inches high.
I know I can reach the sky!

I get nutrients from the earth.
In its ground I had my birth.
Sky Water helps me to grow.
I need it often. This I know.

What I like best is the Sun.
In it I feel like a 'Special One.'
Its rays warm me with its love.
They come from high above.

This routine is simple but sure.
I do not really need much more.
I turn toward its sweet light.
It is always my pure delight.

Does God do the same for you?
Please tell me, if you like to.
I love to hear of His loving care.
Of His loving ways I am aware.

Was He the cause of your birth?
Does He give you water for life?
How tall will your height be?
Will you be taller than little me?

You surely must feel His Sun.
It is unmistakably the only One.
Without it wouldn't life be lacking?
With it He assures His 'backing.'

I help neighbors that fly around.
They have a 'buzzzzing' sound.
Are you kind to those near you?
I think our Maker wants us to.

We have so much in common.
Life is so grand. It's not solemn.
God dresses me in my attire.
His ways are so much higher.

I am happy where He planted me.
His flower is all that I want to be.
He knows my needs before I ask.
Here comes the Sun. Time to bask!

"Walk on Water"

You probably know me as Peter.
Some have called me their leader.
I want to share a story that's true.
This could have happened to you.

I remember looking into His eyes.
A Master's gaze has no disguise.
He said, "Come," looking at me.
With piercing eyes He could see.

I left the boat. On water I walked.
I did not hesitate, but soon I balked.
For some reason I lost my nerve.
Things in life cause us to swerve.

Looking back I remember that wind.
And the water swirling did me offend.
Instead of focusing on His Word
I succumbed to fear; that's so absurd.

He can calm any raging windy sea,
Especially those within you and me.
My faith in Him He hoped to build.
He knew that in Him I am fulfilled.

If you should panic and start to sink,
Call, "Save me, Lord." Don't even think.
Don't get distracted by circumstances.
Trust always in Him. Take no chances.

He is your Leader, Lord, and Savior.
He talks to you who have found favor.
His Heavenly Father is your Father too.
They Two are God and They love you.

Later I did receive power from on High.
The Holy Spirit really helped me get by.
He will empower you with faith galore.
"Lord help them to follow You more."

"Hourglass of Poetry"

When I turn over an hourglass
On the table
I am then able
to see sand goes through fast.

The grains of sand are
Like the thoughts in 'thar'
Going from my brain to my mind.
That is how I get 'rhyme in time.'

It is better, some say,
Thoughts come that way,
A little idea at a time.
To help my thoughts refine.

It would be a bit much
If they came all in one bunch.
Just like food for the body
One bite at a time we munch.

It seems that a lot today
Is the same in that way.
I think the key word is flow.
With poetry it can be slow.

Some thoughts come in a blast.
My hand has to move very fast.
In the back room of my mind
I have to store them in time.

How it works is really fine.
It is all connected to time.
Seconds flow in their unwind,
Making words that rhyme.

The Hourglass of poetry
Brings words through time.
My poems are somewhere
In there to be unlocked with care.

"Blessed Lambs for Him Wait"

We are just little lambs.
He is The Great I Am.
Near Him we are docile
And He gives us our smile.

We are part of His flock.
Together we walk and talk.
His Son we've heard
And follow The Word.

Jesus is our Shepherd.
Him, have you heard?
You are really missing
Unless you too listen.

Goats are over there.
They do not care.
Going their own way
They waste their day.

Lambs dote on His Word.
Goats think it's absurd.
They'll buck with horns.
You, they might scorn.

We stay away from them
Separated at day's end.
Our way is to show love.
We aim for Heaven above.

We try to share jour joy
Pure with no ploy.
If the world overwhelms,
We are blessed in His realm.

The Lamb of God reigns.
Some show Him disdain.
Oh, you, hard-hearted
Please don't be parted!

Him, would you like to see?
One day you can be
Inside Heaven's Gates.
Blessed Lambs, for Him wait.

"Disciple's Light"

I will follow You, Lord, on this earth.
You knew that though before my birth.
Your way of doing things is for me.
To my life Your Light adds ecstasy.

Your Light christens me every day.
It insures that on Your path I stay.
I walk with You in Your Holy Presence.
Your Light purifies me free of offence.

Who'd I follow, if I didn't follow You?
To Your words I will always be true.
They are my Manna for nourishment,
And Water for graceful replenishment.

I feel the warmth of Your Son-Shine.
I realize that I am following The Divine.
You motivate with a loving Godly Grace.
In that Light we move at the same pace.

In our union we stay continually free.
"I love You; You love me" is our polity.
People of the world seek after treasure.
Give me Your 'Pearl' without measure!

You had twelve disciples, that's true.
They showed us how to follow You.
I will pray and ask for daily guidance.
Light shine for my complete reliance.

Lord, give me the Grace to excel.
Human interest from me, do repel.
I want to shine for You just right.
Keep me in Your Disciple's Light.

Anointed and ready, so humbly I go.
Living with others in earth's 'show.'
There is so much good for me to do,
In a Disciple's Light daily with You.

"Mirror"

Mirror, you never change.
The reflection of me
Is always there.
Maybe I am you.

Maybe you are me.
No, I am in you.
Is that an image I see?
Or is that really me?

Oh, image that I see
Are you really me?
Your left arm is my right.
My right arm is your left.

Your left side looks right.
My right side looks left.
Is it a trick that I see?
Will you go, if I count to 3?

Image, you are here to stay.
With you I like to play.
You are always faithful.
You appear every day.

Sky reflects water;
Water reflects sky.
What if we go
Really high?

Heaven above
Earth below
Which is the mirror
I want to Know?

God above
Man below
We are Your Image.
So this I know.

Do I see You
When I see me?
Am I in You?
Are You in me?

Do I reflect you
As you made me?
I am amazed
Still in a daze!

This turned out profound
The long way around.
The image for me is
What turned out to be this.

"Only In Him"

If everyone knows everything,
Or At least they think they know,
Aren't they taking away something
From God 'running the show?'

Let's go easy and go slow.
He changes so-so's to a glow.
What am I talking about?
Turn to Him Who has 'clout.'

You know what I mean.
There is no in-between.
From "baby stuff" we wean.
Upon His Word we are keen.

Depending on Him for progress.
Let us not even slightly regress.
Our salvation depends on Him.
He has taken away our sins.

Let us begin anew to do
What is pleasing and true.
Everyone knows he should.
Only in Him are we good.

"I Surrender All"

Take my senses, they are yours.
Take my hands for your chores.
My feet are for spreading good news.
I gain in Christ the more self I lose!

Make my life a living love-sacrifice.
I give to You joyfully without strife.
Anoint me with all-consuming love
Blessing me in the form of a Dove!

I want to be a yielded vessel for You.
Light my path with blessed things to do.
I pick up my cross and live Your way
Giving of myself willingly day after day!

It is no longer I who in this body lives.
It is Christ who true life to me He gives.
As You surrendered your life for the world,
Let my surrendered life in You be unfurled!

In the Garden Adam and Eve had it all.
You had to give Your all after their fall.
You are the New Adam, God's Son.
In You we who surrender all are One!

I surrender all for you, My God, My Lord!
I am Your child. I lay down my sword.
I die to self daily so You may live in me.
Thank You for dying and making me free!

"Faith He Loves"

When He returns
Love we earn
By being faithful
For Our Wonderful!

Will He find
The loving kind
For Him waiting
Faithfully anticipating?

Faith He loves.
It is from above.
In our hearts
It never parts.

For Him look.
Read His Book.
He is True.
You be too.

Why wait more?
Him we adore.
In our hearts
He lives evermore!

"It Is You Who"

It Is You Who can make a sunrise.
It Is You Who knows Heaven's size.

It Is You Who can fill the landscape.
It Is You Who brings darkness's drape.

It Is You Who gives sunset its glow.
It Is You Who unveils nature's show.

It Is You Who knows the ocean's deep.
It Is You Who gives joy for us to keep.

It Is You Who I am living my life for.
It Is You Who knows what is in store.

It Is You Who knows Santa's Prancer.
It Is You Who has all of the answers.

It Is You Who gives men their breath.
It Is You Who knows the time of death.

It Is You Who gives us truly good things.
It Is You Who walks on Saturn's Rings.

It Is You Who loves Your Begotten Son.
It Is You Who planned sin to be undone.

It Is You Who is the world's True Light
It Is You Who does things always right.

"The Beauty of the Earth" - A Hymn

I thank God for the beauty of the Earth.
Upon man He has crowned His Worth.
His might is reflected in mountains high.
They all point to His Majesty in the sky.

Creatures inhabit swelling surging seas.
They praise Him reflecting His Bounty.
His Invisible Love for Earth we can see.
He clothes the trees with its greenery.

I thank God for the beauty of the Earth.
Upon man He has crowned His Worth.

Flowers and Autumn Leaves' Colors
Flash seasonal glory one after another.
We can learn, if we listen to the animals
Of God's Sovereign Dominion over all.

He makes rapid rivers flow to their end.
Silver rains and sunshine He does send.
As trees and mountains rise to The Son,
We raise our arms to Our Beautiful One.

I thank God for the beauty of the Earth.
Upon man He has crowned His Worth.
His might is reflected in mountains high.
They all point to His Majesty in the sky.

I thank God for being made in His Image.
Jesus to Heaven has given safe passage.
The Earth was created for us to be in Him.
So we raise voices in praise in this hymn.

I thank God for the beauty of the Earth.
Upon man He has crowned His Worth.

"Lord, I Love You"

In the morning, Lord, You are on my mind.
The cares of the world, Your Care will refine.
Today, Father, take me under Your Wing.
I am praying that You will lead in everything.

People ask me, "Why do you love God so?"
I just say, "It's His love. That's all I know."
Why do I need You like I do?
Lord, I can't live without You.

There is one thing that I know for sure.
Lord, I love You more and more.
When church bells ring all over town,
I hear a 'We Worship You, Lord' Kinda-Sound.

All of my friends wonder what I've found.
Please loose all of those that are bound.
I hope that Your Grace increases to abound.
You deserve always to be gloriously renown.

May children grow up with lips praising You.
I know that Your Love will guide them too.
As the years of wisdom pass day by day,
May words of loving praise be what we say.

In the evening, Lord, You are on my mind.
The cares of the world seem so far behind.
Today You have taken me under Your Wing.
Thank You for leading me in everything.

"Lift Me Up"

Lift me up to where the Eagles soar.
Lift me up to Your Throne to adore.

Lift me up when I am feeling down.
Lift me up with You being around.

Lift me up on A Soft Angel Wing.
Lift me up to hear the stars sing.

Lift me up in the glow of the Moon.
Lift me up to be ever with You soon.

Lift me up where Your Grace begins.
Lift me up where victory In You wins.

Lift me up to ride a shooting star.
Lift me up to spread Your love far.

Lift me up where I can breathe of You.
Lift me up so Your Will I can pursue.

Lift me up in the month of May.
Lift me up every month, every day.

Lift me up on This Good Earth
Lift me up to celebrate new birth.

Lift me up to ride a comet's tail.
Lift me up where men do not fail.

Lift me up to be with The Great I Am.
Lift me up to be with His Dear Lamb.

"Beauty Is Love, and Love Is God"

Mix love and beauty and you have Our Loving God.
He shows His love in the earth's & sky's loveliness.
Use *spiritual eye* to see and it won't seem so odd.
Seeing God in things eliminates human loneliness.

Set your sight on 'Things Above' and His Pure Love.
While on Earth, we can glimpse His Heavenly Glory.
We see in part, but we will see fully in Glory above.
Each of us will share our story of His Beauty & Love.

Beauty rests in the faith-filled eyes of the beholder.
Jesus has the love that makes us live our life bolder.
His Beauty radiates joy and welcoming love to all.
Humbly prostrate yourself before Him; do not stall.

His apostles were overwhelmed in His Radiant Light,
Transfiguring Himself beautifully beyond human sight.
His beauty is beyond any God-Created celestial star.
Wise men do seek His Beauty and Love near and far.

Beauty Is Love, and Love Is God is realized in Grace.
It is His Beautiful Love that renews our Human Race.
What would we do without His Beautiful Love Divine?
It is The Light that perfects our frail dross and refines.

Set your sight on 'Things Above' and His Pure Love.
While on Earth, we can glimpse His Heavenly Glory.
We see in part, but we will see fully in Glory above.
Each of us will share our story of His Beauty & Love.

"Anointed Zest"

Add some zest! Add some zest!
That lively quality brings the best.
Look around! Look up and down!
Add some real zing around town.

Come joyfully alive! Come alive!
Give your neighbors a 'high five.'
Our Jesus is Why! Jesus is Why!
Give His Saving Grace a real try.

Do not take His love for granted.
In Christ's Anointing be planted.
You can surely pass life's tests.
Live for Christ in Anointed Zest.

Grace adds zest! Add That Zest!
Seek It and add It to all the rest.
You will be happy! Hands clappy!
Your dancing feet will be happy.

So come on now! Come alive!
Give your neighbors a 'high five.'
Tell them just why! Jesus is Why!
Give His Saving Grace a real try.

Do not take His love for granted.
In Christ's Anointing be planted.
You can surely pass life's tests.
Live for Christ in Anointed Zest.

"My Child, Let Me In"

My Child, open the door of your heart; let Me in.
From there, I do not ever want to part from within.
Let Me shower blessings on you of My Sweet Grace.
Open wide the arms of your soul and, Me, embrace,

In the heart Divinity and humanity marvelously collide,
Your heart is a haven where I will mysteriously abide.
We will experience The Father's All-Consuming Love.
We will be One in His Magnificent Light from above.

How much I loved you from the start; you will realize.
The Clear Light in your eyes will show no soul disguise.
The Joy you share will cause frowns to erase.
I will put The Bright Glow of Wisdom upon your face.

Open wide the arms of your soul and, Me, embrace.
Let Me shower blessings on you of my Sweet Grace.
From You, I do not ever want to part from within.
My Child, open the door of your heart; let Me in.

"Your Love"

Your Love can make a blind man see.
Your Love can make a disease history.

Your Love can make the birds migrate.
Your Love can make the Earth rotate.

Your Love can make water into wine.
Your Love can make wholeness mine.

Your Love can make everything bright.
Your Love can make me have insight.

Your Love can make the sky be blue.
Your Love can make old things new.

Your Love can make the Red Sea part.
Your Love can make happy days start.

Your Love can save everyone's soul.
Your Love can sustain the very old.

Your Love can make a mountain move.
Your Love can make sin be removed.

Your Love can make doubt be resolved.
Your Love can make problems be solved.

Your Love can cause people to accept.
Your Love can cause men to respect.

Your Love can cause planets to rotate.
Your Love gave us Jesus to imitate.

Your Love gave us hope at The Cross.
Your Love has redeemed the lost.

Your Love gave The Spirit to teach.
Your Love puts Heaven within reach.

Your Love brought Jesus in the manger.
Your Love makes no man a stranger.

Your Love came in the form of a man.
Your Love gave us Salvation's Plan.

Your Love fills me with exceeding joy.
Your Love is meant for girls and boys.

Your Love came to Planet Earth.
Your Love gives men New Birth.

Your Love, give me without measure.
Your Love is my sought-after treasure.

"Life Is A Road Trip to Heaven"

Life is a short road trip to heaven.
Traveling in His Light is a 'given.'
No bags needed for the flight out.
Proceed boldly without a doubt.

The Lord will be your Guiding Star
Lighting your path wherever you are.
He provides manna with His Word.
Share with those who have not heard.

Stop at waypoints along the way.
They can add meaning each day.
The poor, hungry, and down trodden
Are sights not soon to be forgotten.

Gather memories along your way.
Glimpse God's Hand filling the day.
Blessings in life keep you enamored
As you go forth spiritually armored.

No need to look back as you journey.
To this earthly life you are not returning.
Set your inner sight on Heaven above.
God awaits with All-Consuming Love!

You are traveling in a 'Bubble of Grace,'
A special vehicle for the human race.
Powered by His Sacrifice for His Chosen
Determined beforehand who goes in.

I hope to see you one blessed fine day
At our journey's end where we will stay
Blessed in His Overwhelming Presence
Offering our lives to Him as our present!

"All We Ask"

All We ask is that You bring all to Christ.
Lord, give those seeking spiritual sight.
Life is short, but, God, Your Love is long.
Bring them to You, where they belong!

Lord, unmask life's illusion and delusion.
It is You that they should be choosin'.
All of them are seeking real freedom.
Increase their faith and redeem them.

We ask this, Father, and never do doubt.
Only You can bring men's good about.
It is not too much for your child to ask.
For You it is a marvelous simple task.

Jesus asked for disciples that He knew.
Lord, we ask for those who love Jesus too.
We are to be part of The Bride of Christ,
A truth that is paramount in Thy Sight.

Lord You told us that we ask and receive.
In Thy Holy Word we adamantly believe.
The plight of man's fall You understand.
We ask and wait for Thy Merciful Hand.

"Fill Up My Day, Oh Lord"

Fill up my day with abiding in You.
It is a blessed way and easy to do.
I choose to be in Your company, Oh Lord.
I surrender and lay down my sword.
Fill up my day, Oh Lord!
Fill up my day, Oh Lord! Fill it with You!

Fill up my day, Oh Lord
I have come to rely upon You,
To fill my day with things to do.
You are the reason for my living.
My whole life for you I am giving!
Fill up my day, Oh Lord!
So fill up my day, Oh Lord! Fill it with You!

On the sea of life people are tossed around,
With no anchor of faith to hold them down.
You bring light into my life each day,
And fill up my life with You in every way.
Fill up my day, Oh Lord!
Fill up my day, Oh Lord! Fill it with You!

Fill up my day, Oh Lord
Come, Lord, let me feel Your Presence.
Make me want more of Divine Essence.
Fill me with 'Heavy Duty Stuff' today.
Only Your Grace can fill me this way!
Fill up my day, Oh Lord! Fill it with You!

Fill up my day, Oh Lord
I have come to rely upon You,
To fill my day with things to do.
You are the reason for my living.
My whole life for you I am giving!
So fill up my day, Oh Lord!
Fill up my day, Oh Lord! Fill it with You!

"You Are the Way"

I am the light.
You are the light.
Christ is the Light
In you and me...

Grace is the way.
It frees us today.
No more sin to pay.
We are free...

All I want to do is be in YOU...
All I want to do is live for YOU...
Night and day...

Oh... Oh... Oh... Show me the way...
Oh... Oh... Oh... Show me the way...Oh, Lord.
Oh ...Oh... Oh ...Lord You are The Way...

"As Easy As 1, 2, Free"

Lord, in You I want to be.
It is as easy as 1, 2, Three.
Faith in You sets me free
To abide always in Thee.

In Your Light I now see.
I am one in Thy Trinity
I in You, You in me
In the Father we will be.

To You I bow my knee
For what You did for me.
You have made me worthy
To be with You for eternity.

1, 2, Three, Grace is free.
Abiding in it is the key.
More of You, less of me,
You bless me remarkably.

Being in You One, Two, 3
Makes me so very happy.
Holy Spirit leads constantly,
Sealing me in You, Three.

In Christ I have my victory.
It is as easy as 1, 2, Three.
Father, Son, Holy Spirit, 3
In One, all abiding in me.

Your Presence is so lovely.
It is free and easy as 1, 2, 3.
It overwhelms me completely.
Your life You share with me!

Oh how marvelous it is to be
Walking with Thee continually.
Your love quickens me daily,
Before I can count 1, 2, Free!

"A Dark World in Need of Light"

Our world is in need of Our Father's Light.
We must all pray for His spiritual insight.
What does understanding the atom count
If we reject Jesus' Sermon on the Mount?

The world has achieved scientific brilliance
Without exhibiting true Godly Conscience.
Countries have become nuclear giants
Demonstrating behavior of ethical infants.

God has not called His children to isolate.
He has called us to go boldly and infiltrate.
It is possible to impact the world for Christ.
We do not have to compromise what's right.

God will protect us always from the evil one.
He has poured out His love to us in His Son.
We are not of the world and its 'dark ways.'
A life of Light flows from The Ancient of Days.

If Heaven is what we want some day to obtain,
Keep the eternal rules Heaven has ordained.
A world of Light starts in each of our hearts.
By shining God's Light we each do our part.

"One in Your Marvelous Light!"

Everything will be revealed in You
For you unite all things anew.
In Your Peaceful, Graceful Light
We are One in You, Oh Lord.
We are One in Your Marvelous Light!

Men try to make things seem new.
They use their minds to try to do.
In You we have complete victory.
It is Your Light In and upon me
That makes me holy in Thee!

You are A Holy God, The Mighty I Am.
There is nothing that You cannot do.
It is marvelous how You make us One
Through The Blood of Your Precious Lamb!
He is The Light, The Holy One, Your Son!

It is That Marvelous Light that I love
Shining down on me from above.
That Light keeps me free in Thee,
And enables me to live Godly for Thee.
Holy I am in It, and that is what You see!

Thank You, Heavenly King On High,
To give life to me, You chose to die.
I will Live my life In The Light for You.
I will take up the cross and follow too.
It is the very least Your Son can do!

"We Are in Awe"

We are being governed by our passions
As we go around seeking life's attractions.
Shed Your Gospel Light in glorious array.
Guide us so that we do not go far astray.

Your marvelous moral maxims fill our mind
Like a battalion of a celestial army so divine.
Your words have a secret virtue and efficacy
That stops at nothing to enable one to see.

Your manner of convincing has no comparison.
Everything astonishes about Christ, Your Son.
You gather us into Your bosom, our true country
Where we will have fulfillment as Your family.

You teach us about having life for all eternity
And prove it by sharing with us Your Divinity.
No greater love has anyone ever showed us.
Our praises are going to You dawn to dusk.

You are our Father, truly our God and Friend
Promising to be with us for a life without end.
We are in awe of You for what You have done.
Your Truth embraces the universe In Your Son.

"The Master Baker"

My breakfast bread is a Godly creation.
It's a slice of life spread with inspiration.
Sometime it contains things that I see.
Other times ideas well up inside of me.

I sit patiently and wonder what it will be.
It always seems to appear magically.
I write the thoughts down as they come.
With lightning speed it is always done.

My words all line up in an orderly flow
Rhythmic and non-stop, row after row.
Ingredients I use are a different kind
Mixed in heaven and baked in my mind.

In this fast-pace electronic human race
It is easy to forget about God's Grace.
It is a free connection to The One above,
The Master Baker, Who bakes with love!

Finished loaf placed on my heart's shelf,
It was done with His Help, not by self.
It is marked with a cross for all to see.
This work was done by Him, not me.

"Another Day"

I am thankful for another day.
A day I can to You pray.
Today You show me the way.
Another day in You I stay.

The birds in the air depend on You.
They wait upon Your loving care.
The fish in the water down deep
Rely on You for them to keep.

Plants grow from seeds we sow.
Animals multiply with love just so.
Each living thing on Earth knows
Another day in Your care smoothly goes.

Everything You created on a special day.
Some wonder if it happened that way.
I like the way You did it day by day.
For You it was just another day.

If you give me another day,
I think I would like to repay
Your love for me some way.
All it would take is another day.

"Photos, the Windows of Time"

There was no window above the mantel,
But had a view where she could see well.
She stood looking at pictures all in a row.
My, the years passed and she did grow!

In the first picture she held Dad's hand.
Thank you, Dad, for being a good man.
Next picture she's in that satin blue dress.
Thanks, Mom, for always knowing best!

The years in college went by so very fast.
She was posing in cap and gown at last.
It wasn't long before 'bells were ringing,'
A framed memory of her heart singing!

Then the sweet fruits of life came to be,
A picture of each child, one, two, three.
To her these meant more than life itself.
For sure, they belonged on this top shelf.

As she stood gratefully looking at these,
She smiled looking at them so pleased.
They were like reflections of life sublime,
She saw gazing through the windows of time!

She thanks God for what had come before.
And grateful for what He would have in store.
There is always room for a few pictures more,
Of the things in her life that she is thankful for!

"Fifty Lacking Five"

And Abraham spoke to The Lord about His plan.
Referring to the devastation soon to be at hand.
Would Sodom be spared if 50 righteous be found?
The Lord's mercy again and again would resound.

"Suppose that the fifty righteous are lacking five.
Will You destroy the whole city because of five?"
He said, "I will not destroy it, if I find there forty-five."
For them He would keep all inhabitants there alive.

Abraham asked God a number again and again.
The Lord responded with leniency toward men.
40 righteous therein would get response the same
Even 30, 20 and 10, but it was serious, not a game.

As we know Sodom and Gomorrah were not spared.
The fumes of fire and brimstone filled the valley air.
God's wrath was toward the unrighteous and unjust.
Judgements upon man's evil will come as God dost.

We are all but mere men made of ashes and dust.
Store up good in heaven, safe from moth and rust.
His lovingkindness is toward Children of Abraham.
Trust in the Lord's Ways and live forever. Amen.

"Weak and a Way"

All of mankind is weak and needs a way
To find assurance for itself for a better day.
We have adorned our physical exteriors
To cover up our being interior inferiors.

This goes way back to Adam and Eve
Hiding nakedness and having to leave.
Inside they had lost their Divine Essence.
They lost it within, and lost His Presence.

Then comes along Jesus Christ, hooray!
He came to save, saying, "I Am The Way."
In our weakness Grace makes us strong.
With God's newly anointed we do belong.

There is no need to feel alone and down
Turn to Him. Your answer will be found.
He will raise you up. You will surely soar.
Inside you will feel good like a lion's roar!

Don't take my word for it. Take His Word.
Thank The Lord for the Gospel you heard.
He will bless you to stay on a lighted path
That leads to eternal bliss, not God's wrath!

"The World Is Unaware"

If you have a need, turn to Jesus.
He is ready always to please us.
He doesn't want you to be without.
Use your faith and have no doubt.

There is so much going on today.
Don't forget though He's The Way.
He will cause your faith to grow.
We all need to adhere to Him so.

The world offers you a sensual life.
He offers you peace without strife.
His blessing you can't compare.
Of its value the world is unaware.

He will guide you along life's path.
In the midst of trouble you'll laugh.
Get ready to serve and do His will.
Expect His Holy Spirit, you to instill.

Have no fear for He is in control.
He'll cast you in life's starring role.
Do your best relying on His Grace.
Stay the course and win the race.

"A Vessel of Your Love"

Give me another day to do,
Lord, to show that I love You.
Even though I do not see You,
I can love those whom I do.

I will give You a little kindness, and
When I give my fellow man a hand,
It is You that will be receiving when
I show others love they understand.

In the eyes of a hungry child,
I see your look meek and mild.
The old man I meet down the street,
Is really You that I see and greet.

Let Your Presence be on all today
Who pass my way, to show them
Your Grace in a very special way,
Without words that I need not say!

I want to be a vessel of love for You,
To be used by You in whatever I do.
Let all be blessed by Your Light,
So they can see You are their delight!

"It All Adds Up"

We're the sum of what we've done.
The tally sheet started on day one.
Records are kept in heaven in books
Up high where nothing He overlooks.

We all desire a golden winner's cup.
In the end we'll know. It all adds up.
Crowns and rewards pile up on high
Secure in a heavenly bank in the sky.

The rule book, God's Word, the Bible
Teaches that we all go the extra mile.
Adhere to it without fail until life's end.
The rules are clear. They do not bend.

Christ has made our burden very light.
The desires of His heart is our delight.
Grace makes it possible to live in Him.
Our hearts keep singing a joyful hymn.

Faith carves His Jesus Masterpiece.
The Sculptor gives our form release.
His finger carved 10 Commandments
Placed in us where they were meant.

As children we learned to count to ten.
We did this to please our parents then.
The bottom line of our life's sum total:
A life lived for Christ is so worth it all.

"Lord Help Me Today"

Lord strengthen me today.
Show me the way
To please You
In all that I do.

Let Your Grace
Rest upon the human race.
Enable us to stay
In Your Light today.

Abide in me lastingly true,
As I abide in You.
I will know what to do
With help from You.

Uphold me all day through
In all that I do.
For I love you,
And You love me too.

"Do What Is Blessed"

If you're not blessed,
Let that something rest.
You should be happy,
Not feeling down and sappy.

Being down is a sign
To wait for another time,
Or a different thing find.
Being happy is a good sign.

This is an innate rule,
Not often taught in school:
To do what's best
Do what is blessed.

Your decisions you'll learn
Should be 'Light Discerned.'
They should be with ease.
You should feel joy and peace.

It is an art to live in the Light.
A smile is a pleasing sight.
It will be on your face.
A frowny face it will replace.

O God, be My Guiding Light
To do what's pleasing in Your sight.
If You are happy, I will be too.
I want to be in The Light with You.

"Try a Little Courage"

When the words of people get you down,
Try a little courage, that's what I found.
If the things in life thwart you like a vicious hound,
Try a little courage, that's what I found.
If your way of living is being threatened & unwound,
Try a little courage, that's what I found.
If ethical morals seem to be drowned,
Try a little courage, that's what I found.

When the winds of opposition press you down,
Try a little courage, that's what I found.
When ghosts and goblins seem all around,
Try a little courage, that's what I found.
When the dragons of old seem to be in town,
Try a little courage, that's what I found.

For whatever needs earned or whatever unbound,
Try a little courage.
That's what I've learned, and that's what I found.

If ever a fear or hindrance resounds,
Try a little courage, that's what I found.
If the earth around you is crumbing down,
Try a little courage, that's what I found.

If ever a bad situation needs turned,
Try a little courage, that's what I learned.
If justice and truth need to be earned,
Try a little courage, that's what I learned.

For whatever needs earned or whatever unbound,
Try a little courage.
That's what I learned, and that's what I found.

"God Is There"

God will show you a way outstanding.
Stop relying on your own understanding.
There is only one way to know for sure.
Don't flip a coin. Get your knees on the floor.

Tired of spinning your wheels today?
Need a rest from all the restless days?
Don't dismay. Hope is on the way.
Turn your face to Heaven and pray.

Have you come to a dead end in your doings?
Can't figure out how to turn it about?
Call on The One up above and stop stewing.
He will show you the best way without a doubt.

When you can't seem to make ends meet,
And you can't seem to find that job you need.
Don't stand in that line. Find time for The Divine!
He will save you just in time.

Are you wandering around aimlessly?
Need a place to go to ponder hopefully?
Try going to a church nearby.
It is more than a steeple reaching the sky.

Don't worry. Don't dismay.
God is there. Come what may.
He will help you in tough times.
He will show you the way.

"God in Space"

It is You, Lord, Who sits upon the circle of the Earth.
It is You, Lord, Who hangs the Earth upon nothing.
You are the Creator Who gave the universe its birth.
You are our Father Who holds together everything.

Some men have had the thrill of walking on the moon.
They probably thought nothing could top this very soon.
They saw that the Glory of God was declared in space,
A serendipitous result of taking part in the space race.

The Apollo Astronauts had moments of crowning glory.
The Crowns that Jesus gives will last throughout eternity,
Tarnishing and fading not, but space and time, it outlasts.
One is the result of a rocket, the other a Trumpet Blast.

In the days of Our Lord waters were braved by fishermen.
He caused them to bear much fish of the Sea of Galilee.
Apart from You we can do nothing today as it was then.
Today, we must conquest the realm of space for Thee.

When we consider the Heavens, the work of Thy Fingers,
The comfort of having You as Father in our soul lingers.
The moon and the stars, which You have wisely ordained
Is a testimony in space that this greatness is Your Domain.

"Healing the Vexed and Perplexed"

Only Christ can heal someone's heart that is vexed.
He's the answer for a world that's perplexed.
Only God's Son teaches love for our brother.
The world can change, if we love one another.

Science has a helpful influence in our society.
Its answers give us certain intellectual sobriety.
It does not teach personal Godly responsibility.
Though useful, it does not strengthen morality.

We need the inner strength of Our God's Grace.
With it we have the conscious presence of Him.
Christ truly is The Solver for a frail human race.
Without Him man attempts to solve on his whim.

A world of hate seeks its own for advancement.
What it needs is God's Love for its development.
Problems will arise from being in that contention.
Only The Comforter quells with loving affection.

"Opportunity Knocks"

Not everyone has opportunity for notability,
Nor is someone likely to become a celebrity.
Opportunity is given for us to walk with One
Who brings new life being God's loved Son.

Not many have saved up millions in banks,
Nor have many joined society's elite ranks.
However we can have in our heart thanks.
God saved us from sin to which we sank.

Men spend billions to secure world peace.
Many have spent gold for captive's release.
Walking with Jesus is free by Faith's Grace,
A gift of God, not our works, as is the case.

You do not have to go to Mars or the Moon.
You can find Salvation's Light in your room.
You do not have to walk across the country
To start A Jesus Walk for eternity that's free.

"Lower Down Your Bucket"

Along life's journey we may encounter doldrums.
Do not be discouraged; parched days will come.
Lower your bucket down in the Living Jesus Well.
Join the countless stories his children have to tell.

Lower it down; bring up Water Living and Eternal.
Drink and share Jesus' lasting life that is Paternal.
Are you still having dry days; are the winds still?
Fill your day with prayer and fasting for God's will.

Soon you'll be sailing full sail in an anointed breeze.
Abide in Christ and get through the day with ease.
Lower your bucket into your Well of Faith as needed.
Bring up Grace that refreshes your Godly life indeed.

Lower down your bucket among those who believe.
Bring up God's love for others to your awareness.
Grace and mercy He has given to many to relieve.
He extends His salvation with peace and kindness.

"Happy Instruments of Turning"

The Lord's sifting of all people is endless.
He sends choice grain into the wilderness.
His Just Hands make happy instruments,
Turning many from lives of bewilderment.

Victory in Christ gives man sacred rights.
We share Gospel's doctrine, Love's Proof.
We are ambassadors shining Bright Lights,
Shining knowledge and love of the truth.

Let us all unite to help our fellow man decide.
May Christ's Gospel be embraced worldwide.
The Earth be filled with the Lord's Knowledge.
All called by the Lord's Grace will acknowledge.

Casting ourselves in faith at our Master's Feet,
We are available instruments for evil's defeat.
Empowered by atonement of Our Redeemer,
Immortality comes from The Master Schemer.

The Wonderful Gospel of The Prince of Peace
Is the only sure hope of the world's real release.
Let us be happy instruments for all men turning
By sharing the Light for which they are yearning.

"Delving Deep"

Lord, Your mysteries I want to pursue.
I see the physical and I glimpse You.
Oh, Deep Oceans, what do you contain?
Oh, Lord, make knowledge of You plain!

How marvelous are Your Secret Ways!
You keep our soul thirsting and ablaze.
Grace, our soul in You does breathe.
Your Anointing upon us we do receive.

The deeper I go, more of Grace I know.
The more about Your Grace that I know,
The more Love to me You kindly show.
I am deep in You; this I wonderfully know.

Men explore the deep sea's mysteries.
They consider it the next frontier to see.
I delve deeper into Your Eternal Being.
More of Your Glory I hope to be seeing.

Your Blessing keeps us in You abiding.
In Your Light our old self has no hiding.
All is revealed in The Light of Christ.
Faith gives us that special inner sight.

Delve deep into the ocean and universe.
But explore God's Word verse by verse.
It is good to do both, but not in reverse.
Pursue mysteries of earth; be in You first.

Go deeper into Christ; die to self more.
He will exalt you; Grace you will score.
Oh Keeper of Our Souls, You we adore.
Abide deep in our hearts forever more.

"There Will Be a Better Day"

If we wait a little longer,
There will be a better day.
God will make you stronger.
The Son will show you the way.

When your thoughts are spinning,
And you are not sure what to do,
Jesus will cause your winning.
The Son will come shining through.

If people around you are unkind,
A friend you need to find.
Don't easily give up hope.
The Lord will help you cope.

When work is getting you down,
An you're tired of this old town,
Keep looking toward the sky.
It is Jesus upon whom you rely.

If your life is full of doubt,
And you just want to sit and pout,
Keep a smile on your face.
Fear His Love will erase.

If you just wait patiently,
There will be a better day.
In His timing you will see.
The Son will show you the way.

What has happened to you
Has happened to others before.
'Out of the blue' you'll know more.
There will be a better day too.

"The Hand You Cannot See"

God orders my world for me.
His hand you cannot see.
It is powerful without a doubt.
Child-like faith can figure it out.

I feel good knowing it is there.
For me Someone really cares.
If it has color, I am not sure.
It is made of Light so pure.

In life His Hand or His Voice
Is used as His Fatherly Choice.
He is in control of our being.
He does so without our seeing.

His hand is there to defend.
There's no need to fend
Don't try to do it on your own.
It is best not to do it alone.

You know It's there by results.
It overturns the world's faults.
Life's mountains move away.
Blue skies replace the gray.

The hand you cannot see
Is always there for you and me.
In it you are safe and free.
In it blessed you will always be.

"Over Life's Seas I Sail to Thee"

Over life's seas as we sail through the years,
We trust and cast upon You all of our fears.
The Captain of our vessel, Sonship, You are.
We sail toward You, Our Bright Morning Star.

In Thee, Jesus, over life's seas I sail to Thee.
In You we are One sailing in Your Spirit free.
It is how it must be, me in You, You in me.
What a blessed journey sailing life's seas!

Sometimes I get real dizzy being with You.
Your Grace makes me a blessing, Lord, too.
Seas present me with challenges often times.
Over mountainous waves, together we climb.

Give me direction, My Marvelous Compass.
Through straits of difficulties help me pass.
Lord, do this always until I arrive at last.
I will sail eternity out of tears of years past.

"The Priceless Boon"

God's Grace upon us is a priceless boon.
My friends receive this not late but soon.
This is Our God's overflowing love to man.
He elevates us like no one else ever can.

Grace in our lives is like a Golden Thread
Sewing for us a blessed life free of dread.
It teaches our children the dignity of man
And individual freedom best, as only it can.

A Heavenly Father gives us Grace's 'edge.'
Against stress and tough times it's a hedge.
Poems have often been written about it.
Grace flows from where The Lord sits.

Oh lost and seeking with a heart yearning,
Embrace The Holy Spirit for your learning.
He guides you into a spiritual treasure vast.
One's soul gladly exclaims, "Lord, at last!"

Our Fathers from time past to Truth adhered.
From this priceless boon they never veered.
It was infused by God into their good hearts
And given to us that we may also be a part.

"Lord, Hold the Door Open"

Hold the door open; I am coming through.
I go to The Father by way of The Door, You.
"I Am The Living Gateway to go to heaven."
"Come through Me. Inherit what I Am given."

Yes, Lord, I see Your arms open wide for me.
From sin's curse I do want to be forever free.
In the world I feel like I am a kind of anomaly.
Entering into You can be done. It's not reverie.

"I, The Welcoming Door, give Heart-Felt Faith.
You are invited to The Wedding of the Lamb.
The Chosen will all be there with The I Am."
Thanks, Lord, for the Words of Life You saith.

Hold The Door open for me; to Thee I do run.
The doors of the world's ways behind I close.
I hope to be among those He loves & knows.
I choose to be saved through God's Only Son.

"Your Blood-Bought Anointing"

Oh, Blessed Redeemer, to You we owe all.
Picturing Our Love on the cross, I do recall.
Your Blood bought Your Precious Anointing.
With this Grace to You, Lord, we are joining.

Your victory on Calvary brought evil's defeat.
Salvation was paid with no need to repeat.
A bridge to The Father, the cross, sufficed.
Your Blood was offered up as Our Sacrifice.

From Heaven The Water of Life does return.
It flows into our hearts freely and unearned.
What we give up of self can't be compared.
For Your Blood-Bought Anointing is so rare.

People put their worth in gold and money.
Give me a spiritual land of milk and honey.
Your Anointing enables me to walk upright
As a child of Yours righteous in Your sight.

"My child, My Shed Blood cleanses of sin."
"Turn to Me; let your new life in Me begin."
I hear Your beckoning, Lord, and I agree.
Your Blood cleanses; Your Anointing frees.

"Connecting Dots"

Through love God is able to reach
From one human being to another.
Only through love, He does teach,
That man is able to help his brother.

How can we say that we love God
Our Father, Whom we do not see,
If our neighbors, we fail to laud,
Who are around, like you and me?

Man's aim is to reach a distant star.
Our fellow man is really not that far.
We seek adventure into outer space.
Needs of others, thrill to embrace.

Helping one neighbor, then another
Is connecting dots of brotherhood.
Love self, then love your brother
Is the way God would, if He could.

"A Life of Light"

A life of Light,
Is pure delight.
Get it right,
A life of Light.

I live by Faith.
I do as He saith.
I walk in His Light
Holy and upright.

The Life of Light,
Is my true delight.
He is Light,
Our Light of Life.

I am one in You.
Grace makes it true.
You have done more
Than anyone before.

I live my life
To please You.
A Lighted Life
Pleases You too.

Light, God gives.
Does He live in You?
I am glad He lives.
I am never blue.

Light makes us right
In God's Sight.
As we live,
Light He does give.

Jesus came
From above,
His aim,
Undying Love.

In Your Light, Oh,
Darkness must go.
You love us so.
Your people know.

"God's Grace"

Refresh me with Living Water.
Your Grace is life for me.
Shelter me in Your Tall Tower.
I seek to abide in Thee.

Lord, You have set me free.
In Your Presence is the place
Where I am meant to be.
Sanctify me with Your Grace.

You make all things new.
I am called to be Your child.
I want to live for You.
Grace is sweet and mild.

Your Word shines brightly.
My soul is illuminated anew.
Forever keep me in Your Light.
I want to be part of You.

Your Grace is heavy upon me
A burden so light and free.
It is heaven's entry fee.
It allows You to be me.

Grace makes all things Light.
I am called to be in you anew.
In that Light everything is right,
Love and Light clear through.

Holy, I am, Lord, in Your Grace.
It is Your gift to the human race
Making us pleasing in Your sight,
So that We may be a pure delight.

"You Save the Day"

Lord, You save the day
In every good way.
I leave it to You.
Me, You renew.

You have a special way
To 'seize the day.'
You do it in a 'Grace Way'
That seems like play.

You save the day.
That is Your saving way.
Whenever I have a need,
You help me with the deed.

In Your Presence I am here
Waiting from You to hear.
The answer comes to me.
In an instant I am free.

If I am wondering what to do,
The answer comes from You.
Words so perfect come to me.
It's amazing. You help me see.

When I am writing, You are too.
You give me thoughts from You.
The right things in a timely way
Come to me about what to say.

You save the day.
It is Your Godly Way.
You save us in every way.
What a Grace filled day!

"Heavenly Magnet"

Plus is up,
Negative is down.
Without a sound
We're closer bound.

A magnet is mysterious.
Does it belong to us?
Did it come from above?
Was it given with love?

Did it come from space,
To help the human race?
Or does it represent another
Godly concept like no other?

Its use is to attract
Some things better.
It might just in fact
Keep us together!

Maybe it is helping us
In the midst of this fuss
To unite mankind
In a Plan Divine.

Wonder what I Am
Talking about then?
Oh, I have attracted
Your attention, and

Imagine this then.
If, God is The Magnet,
His Grace is Its Power
To make us new men
In His redeeming hour.

"One Blessed Day"

One blessed day
I decided to pray.
That was when
You came my way.

My universe was empty.
Life seemed dull.
I reached out
And found life after all.

"Lord bring her to me,"
I prayed on my knees.
One fine day
It came to be.

You were out there,
Meant for me.
I kept believing.
God's Hand I did see.

Now my day is bright
As can be.
One blessed day
His answer came to me.

I am thankful
For that Grace filled day,
The day that
I decided to pray.

It only takes
A moment in time
To fill a day
With something divine.

Now all of my days
Are blessed.
It worked for one.
Why not for the rest?

Since I found her
We pray together.
We use a little faith.
God does it best.

"7eventy-7even"

7eventy-7even reflects God's balancing affinity
For Earth and Heaven that stretches into infinity.
The number seven to God represents fulfilling.
There is just something about it subtly thrilling.

Oh, 7even, what's there about you and Heaven?
Why is it special way up there on Level Seven?
As I look at you, I see in you words, 'even-even.'
Now I am 'On Earth as it is in Heaven' believing.

You look like The Lord's Scale of Just Fulfillment.
Your Will be done in Heaven and Earth as meant.
That is the day Your Glorious Presence resides
And all of Your Children, in You, eternally abide.

Old Adam-New Adam, You did balance the scale.
Eventually to You all men will bow; praise will hail.
Jesus was the 7eventy-7eventh generation's child,
Grace came through Adam's lineage, meek 'n mild.

"Christmas Is Your Day, Jesus"

Christmas is Your day, Jesus.
We celebrate it with You.
"Happy birthday, Jesus,"
Is what we say to You.

This is our way.
The way we give honor that's due.
What a blessed day, Jesus,
The blessing makes all feel new.

We give gifts today, Jesus,
To each other as though to You.
Christmas Is the best day.
Your birthday party we come to.

You showed us a loving way,
A Godly thing to do.
Christmas is here to stay
In the hearts of men who are true.

Of all the days in the year
Christmas is the one so dear.
I wouldn't miss it ever.
It was planned so clever.

Everyone is invited.
We are all so excited.
It is the 'In thing' to do.
It is all because of You!

"Happy Birthday, Jesus!"
What a sweet sound!
The whole world around
Says, "Happy Birthday to You!"

"Born on the First Christmas Day"

Born on the first Christmas Day
Coming in an inconspicuous way
Christ came for sins to pay.
Henceforth, free, man would stay.

Yes, It happened way back then.
The tiny Babe came to us when
Men's hearts were truly yearning
As God's love for man was stirring.

He sent Christ to us, His very best.
It was His only Son, One Blessed,
The Chosen One, to save the rest.
This was the real thing, not a test.

What great love He had for us all.
It started with a child born in a stall.
There is some way we can repay.
Let's give our hearts to Him today.

He was born that Christmas Day.
So we may be born again His way.
"Merry Christmas, Jesus," we say.
We celebrate Your birthday today.

"Snowfall and Jesus on Christmas Eve"

I love snowfall on Christmas Eve.
It is sort of magic; I do believe.

Snowflakes fall gently to the ground
Echoing the silence all around.

Maybe it is how they fall so silently
That fills me with hope so quietly.

The message this evening is peace.
All worldly strife seems to cease.

God's Grace is like snow from above.
It gently fills me with Heavenly Love.

In the silence I feel His Presence
Filling me with Heavenly Essence.

Thank you, Jesus, for Christmas Eve.
You bring real magic for me to believe.

Snowfall and Your Coming are a wonder
On Christmas Eve that I love to ponder.

Thank You for Christmas Eve Snowfall.
Come this Eve, Jesus, and fill us all.

"The Son-Shine Way"

Open the curtain; let the sun shine in.
Do that before the day you begin.
Pause for a moment and let the real
Son shine in; His Grace you will feel.

He is the One that will warm your day.
In Heaven, on Earth, it's the same way.
Don't listen to what other people say.
Just always do it The Son-Shine Way.

You don't need caffeine, ginseng,
Dexedrine, 'bada-bing', or anything.
Let Him be the One about Whom you sing.
Just let the Son show you the real thing.

You got a lot to do and things to say,
Places to go, things to get done,
Errands to run, time for a little fun.
So start your day The Son-Shine Way.

Remember to start your day the Jesus-Way.
Jesus will guide you throughout the day.
Let His Light shine upon you today.
Rest in Him. Do it The Son-Shine Way.

Living like a Christian requires Jesus' Light
To illuminate your path to do it right.
Get ready to do that His Lighted Way.
You got it; do it The Son-Shine Way.

"Love Is a Two-Way Street"

Love is a two-way street.
What you send away one day
Comes back the other way another day
To you to greet and meet.

Send good things down the road to start.
You don't do it for the return,
Or because it's what people earn.
Do it because it is from your heart.

Remember life's highway is not one-way.
Stay to your side for life's ride.
Expect a surprise back on the other side.
Road hogs don't belong on Love's Highway.

The idea can be said in ways that repeat.
What you sow; you shall also reap.
Give and it shall be given to you a heap.
I like, Love is a two-way street.

"Life Stew"

Are you ready to cook?
No need for a cookbook.
At this you are a pro.
The ingredients you know.

We are going to make
A special dish that's new.
A few minutes it will take.
It is A Good Life Stew.

Use what everybody's got.
It's called A Life Pot.
In it you can put a lot.
The taste will hit the spot.

To start put in the best,
Love and happiness,
Faith and success.
It's time for taste test.

It needs Joy and laughter.
Kindness does matter.
Add words that flatter.
Scoop off useless chatter.

Add a pinch of wisdom,
Good works for some,
Money for fun,
And chewing gum!

Put in vacation time,
Learning time,
Howdy-Doody Time,
It's taste time.

Find time to unwind.
Stir in TV time.
Computer is fine,
And time for rhyme.

Now that is out of sight.
You made it just right.
Go ahead take a bite.
Let life take flight.

"Blue Moon"

Blue Moon, you are back so soon.
I love seeing you again too.
You are so full like a big balloon.
Twice this month I saw you!

Some nights, darkness does loom.
You come and take away the gloom.
For you the month makes room,
You rare, 2X's a month full moon!

It is a double dose of your charm.
Or maybe it's some sort of an alarm.
In The Heavens you could be a sign
Of a Second Coming of Another Kind!

"The Altar"

It could be made of stone.
It could be of wood alone.
It can easily be your desk.
It's where time you invest.

The offering is simply you.
The altar is for freely giving,
The best of yourself willing.
It's the pleasing thing to do.

"Those Magic Moments"

Those magic moments I spend with you.
They are grace-filled, making things new.
Your Holy Presence quickens me to do.
I am a docile lamb; my Shepherd is You.

Your anointing upon me keeps me fed.
It is Manna, Your Word, my daily bread.
I am part of Your body; You are my Head.
I am dead to self, but I live in You instead.

Miraculous moments, I think that they are.
You are my Savior, The Bright Morning Star.
Magic is for children with faith like a child.
The magic of Your Loving Grace is so mild.

It transforms me into being someone new.
A person who is one in The Light with You.
It is real life being part of The Majestic One
Who knew me before the world had begun.

"God's Building Blocks of Life"

We all like to build things we like.
It started when we were just tykes.
We stacked blocks to the sky.
I hope a big wind doesn't go by!

Then along came Legos; let's go.
See how many kinds you can build.
We did that until the closet we filled.
And then even the next closet we filled!

In school we learn to build as we sit.
We built friendships so we could fit.
Then of course, we learned the alphabet.
We built words with letters like b-e-t, bet.

Soon we were building muscles that you see,
Trying to be all we could be physically.
That was neat getting to see our form.
We'd come a long way since we were born.

When we were older, we built bolder.
We had gone into the world on our own.
We found a building partner full-grown,
And families we built with love we'd known.

Getting profound, God kind of did the same thing.
He built with fancy chromosome rings,
Connecting them together from nothing.
Now those are some amazing 'building block things!'

Experiences are building blocks, also, we use.
With learning they made the career we choose.
Moment by moment we build what is to be.
Building with blocks God gives us You and Me!

"What Is Life About?"

It is about time.
It is about faith.
It is about Love.
It is about the human race.

Take a look.
Look up.
Look down.
Look all around.

The meaning of life
Have you found?
Pause for a moment.
Does an answer resound?

I could tell you what life is about.
Every man deserves to figure it out.
If you have not, go ahead and start.
You will soon see you are not that smart.

Don't get discouraged; you're not behind,
Sitting and thinking what next to do.
The elusive answer, you may soon find.
Hint: God's Son, Jesus, is a good clue.

We all like a mystery to occupy our mind.
One you are involved in, the solving kind.
You are the author of your own story.
At the end include God's Heavenly Glory.

It is not the end yet, so live with no regret.
Keep looking to the future; the past you'll forget.
It is a non-stop adventure of real-life discovery.
If you stumble along the way, make a recovery.

The further you get in the latter part of life,
The closer you will be to figuring it out.
Just use time wisely, plant seeds of faith,
Show a lot of love. Life? What is it about?

"Whale"

Hail, Oh majestic creature of the sea!
You roam beneath the ocean so free.
How do you know just where to go
In all of that water way down below?

Men have tried to catch you with no avail.
You have brought them in their quest, travail.
Yet every day some make plans to set sail,
And once again, "There she blows," they hail!

You are the mighty invincible powerful whale.
The men all gather lining along the ship's rail
To watch you dive, surface, and see your tail,
And you perform for them freely without fail.

If I could ride you, what a ride that would be,
Bobbing up and down on the back of a whale,
Sowing with the thread of a water wake trail,
The blanket of the ocean that I see around me.

Down under the water's cover slowly we go,
Showing me sights before that I did not know.
You serenade me with a unique sound of "Hello,"
Greeting your friends and family that you love so.

I am amazed at your gentleness and graceful form,
And how bravely you plunge and weather any storm.
Your secret of your greatness men try to understand,
But the only answer is that you're part of God's plan.

Men have tried to use you for their greed and profit.
God used you to bring Nineveh Jonah, His prophet.
I learn how precious you are from days gone by.
I want to ride you to where the water meets sky.

If there ever was a creature that is men's friend,
I think it is you, Big Mighty Friend Until the End.
If you ever have trouble, you I will help defend.
Because for a special creature like you, I will fend.

There are many whale tales that have been told.
They have come to us from the days of old.
This is my tale of a whale; I share with you,
And now it is your whale tale too!

"Read the Writing on the Wall"

There is a saying that is music to my ears.
The words were the same through the years.
It always put a smile on my face.
We were leaders in the industrial race.

I am talking about words that ring true,
"Made in America"; that's what we do.
A trademark of quality, if ever I knew,
We loved to make things brand new.

Whatever happened to that fiery spark
That set hard working Americans apart?
Let us endeavor to get that old habit back
That made us respected leaders of the pack.

With determination through and through,
And help from God, all things we can do.
I know that we can do it; it's true.
We are the Red, White, and Blue.

When the chips are down,
Wipe off that long-faced frown.
Get up and stand in pride.
Defeat, Americans can override.

Remember the war and how we all did rise
To the call to help our nation turn the tide.
We all heard that call from deep inside.
Our country's plea for our aid stirred up pride.

We made things out of nothing almost.
We stopped making a lot of kitchen sinks.
Munitions, planes, and ships were our boast.
We rose to the occasion, a country at the brink.

Recall the Great Depression, so ominous
How it devastated a lot of us.
We rose up out of the mire
To build a nation of people for hire.

I am telling you what we need to do.
I am imploring you to put laziness behind.
A new undefeated attitude we must find.
Victory, like most things, starts within you.

We must no longer adhere to that saying,
"The world owes me a living."
We will get former things back by paying
Our dues to our country by selfless giving.

It is time to rise up dormant you
To the call of greatness, you must pursue.
Let's work together; each doing our part.
For a better America today, we must start.

I have spoken my piece with concern.
It can work; it is something you must yearn.
Wake up and read the writing on the wall,
"For success get started and do not stall."

I am proud of America and so are you.
With firm resolve we must start anew.
With God's help, "Made In America," resounds.
No greater country in the world can be found.

"Heavenly Light Shine on Me"

I am waiting to shine for heaven's sake.
So Heavenly Light shine on me.
I keep waiting, for Your light to shine on me.
Shine, shine, shine, Heavenly Light!
Shine on me! Shine on me!
Heavenly Light shine so people can see.
Let them see, Jesus, that in You we're free.
Shine, shine, Heavenly Light, down on me!
We shine, shine, shine for Thee!
Heavenly Light shine on me!

Out of every moment, the best, I want to make
Here is my life, Lord; it is Yours to take.
Shine, shine, shine, God's Light.
Keep on shining, shining, shining on me!
Heavenly Light shine on me!

Gone are the days of no 'big breaks'
And frail failed human mistakes.
'Cause, Heavenly Light, you shine on me.
Shine, shine, Heavenly Light; keep me free!
Heavenly Light shine, shine on me!

Thank You, Jesus for Your Heavenly Light.
In it, Lord, we follow and do what's right.
We shine, shine, shine for Thee!
Heavenly Light Shine on me!
Keep shining, shining, shining on me!

Out of every moment, the best, I want to make
Here is my life, Lord; it is Yours to take.
Shine, shine, shine, God's Light.
Keep on shining, shining, shining on me!
Heavenly Light shine on me!

This is my Anthem of Hope, and Gladness.
In You Lord, we have fulfillment of happiness.
Shine, shine, shine, Heavenly Light!
Keep on shining, shining, shining on me!
Heavenly Light shine, shine on me!
Heavenly Light shine on me!

"The Spirit of Freedom"

The Spirit of Freedom is not something easily defined.
The Spirit of Freedom reflects one's faith of a Godly Kind.

The Spirit of Freedom does not seek gain for its own.
The Spirit of Freedom adheres to God's Law that is known

The Spirit of Freedom allows us to include God in society.
The Spirit of Freedom seeks activities of a healthful variety.

The Spirit of Freedom helps one's neighbor who has needs.
The Spirit of Freedom increases brotherly love with deeds.

The Spirit of Freedom allows us to pursue our happiness.
The Spirit of Freedom protects our life from undue distress.

The Spirit of Freedom says, "I love you as I love my self."
The Spirit of Freedom gives us the right to be ourselves.

The Spirit of God in all of our lives makes liberty come true.
The Spirit of God guides choices for happiness we pursue.

The Spirit of God gives us our rights to be His Saved Child.
The Spirit of God crowns our lives with Grace that is mild.

The Spirit of Freedom brings The Creators Good for man.
The Spirit of Freedom starts with faith with Bible in hand.

The Spirit of Freedom enables us to develop our interest.
The Spirit of Freedom from our hearts in society is manifest.

The Spirit of Freedom gives us the right to do and say.
The Spirit of Freedom makes for a better blessed day.

The Spirit of Freedom gives us a common conviction.
The Spirit of Freedom unites us in a common devotion.

The Spirit of Freedom allows our faith to be affirmed.
The Spirit of God anoints us to be in Him confirmed.

The Spirit of Freedom saves people from oppression.
The Spirit of Freedom heals people from depression.

The Spirit of Freedom eliminates want for the hurting.
The Spirit of Freedom, a life of poverty, it helps avert.

The Spirit of Freedom is never evil men's unbridled will.
The Spirit of Freedom is not one's pride seeking to fulfill.

The Spirit of Freedom is something every man desires.
The Spirit of Freedom is a dream to which a heart aspires.

The Spirit of Freedom seeks to understand others.
The Spirit of Freedom embraces men of all colors.

The Spirit of Freedom flows from Our Almighty Father.
The Spirit of Freedom is anchored in Jesus, Our Brother.

The Spirit of Freedom cares for the least and the greatest.
The Spirit of Freedom makes our life's fruits the tastiest.

The Spirit of Freedom preserves Liberty's Sacred Fire.
The Spirit of Freedom is always active; it never retires.

The Spirit of Freedom is The Spirit of Him Whom we love.
The Spirit of Freedom reminds us of Lessons from above.

The Spirit of Freedom brings out the hidden good in us all.
The Spirit of Freedom reflects aspirations our heart recalls.

The Spirit of Freedom reflects 'The Law of The Love Giver.'
The Spirit of Freedom flows from Christ like a Mighty River.

Printed in the United States
By Bookmasters